BLACK HISTORY MAKERS

Campaigners

Debbie Foy

WAYLAND

Black History Makers: Campaigners is an introduction to some of black history's most prominent campaigners, all of whom have successfully brought about change. These individuals, with support from their families, friends and followers have time and again proven that by maintaining consistent and constant pressure, change can come – sometimes with violence, bloodshed and loss of life but more often through peaceful measures.

The campaigners in this book have taken the risk that they may be placed in prison, thrown off buses or ridiculed for their beliefs and yet they have kept on fighting. These individuals have endured much suffering so that we can all benefit today and live without fear of being imprisoned for our beliefs, segregated, hounded, beaten or spat at.

The work of campaigners gives us all hope and, as we enjoy the legacies they leave behind, the challenge for you now as you read, listen and observe is to acknowledge that someone risked their life, gave up their freedom and made huge personal sacrifices to bring about change. So, what will you do with your life in exchange?

Mia Morris OBE, Black History Month website

Published in paperback in 2014 by Wayland
Copyright © Wayland 2014

Wayland
Hachette Children's Books
338 Euston Road
London NW1 3BH

Wayland Australia
Level 17/207 Kent Street
Sydney, NSW 2000

Editor: Katie Woolley
Designer: Tim Mayer, MayerMedia
Consultant: Mia Morris OBE, Black History Month website

British Library Cataloguing in Publication Data

Foy, Debbie.
  Campaigners. -- (Black history makers)
  1. Civil rights workers--Biography--Juvenile literature.
  2. Political activists--Biography--Juvenile literature.
  3. Blacks--Biography--Juvenile literature.
  I. Title II. Series
  323.1'0922-dc22

ISBN: 978 0 7502 8857 6

Printed in China

Wayland is a division of Hachette Children's Books,
an Hachette UK company. www.hachette.co.uk

Picture acknowledgements
Bettmann/Corbis: 23TL, Arno Burgi/EPA/Corbis: 23BR, Mary Evans Picture Library/Alamy: 8, Courtesy Everett Collection/Rex Features: 13, 14, 15, Foto24/Gaho Images/Getty Images: 21, Eric Fougere/VIP Images/Corbis: 23C, Ernst Haas/Ernst Haas Collection/Getty Images: 16, Jon Hrusa/EPA/Corbis: 18, Nils Jorgensen/Rex Features: 9, Library of Congress, Washington D.C.: Title page, 6, 10, Wally McNamee/Corbis: 19, Francis Miller/Time-Life Pictures/Getty Images: Contents page, 17, MPI/Getty Images: 7, 11, Gregory Pace/BEI/Rex Features: COVER, 20, Photos 12/Alamy: 23BL, Wisconsin Historical Society/Everett Collection/Rex Features: 12, iStockphoto: 4, Shutterstock: 5, 23

Disclaimer

Words in **bold** can be found in the glossary on page 24.

What is a Campaigner?

Campaigners are people who try to persuade others to change things for the good. Campaigns take place either through public speaking, protests or **petitions**. Campaigners can support civil rights or protest against environmental issues, racism or **oppression**. Most campaigning is peaceful but some can be violent.

Campaigns for freedom

When slavery began in North America in the 1600s, slaves worked for white slaveholders on large **plantations**. They were unpaid and often treated brutally. Between 1600 and 1900, many millions of Africans were shipped to the United States of America (USA) to serve as slaves. Campaigners such as Harriet Tubman (page 7) and the 'Underground Railroad' helped slaves flee the Southern states. **Abolitionists** like Sojourner Truth (page 6) and Frederick Douglass (page 10) devoted their lives to campaigning peacefully against slavery.

Peaceful protests which use non-violence are respected around the world.

THE ERA OF BLACK POWER

The US Civil War of 1861–65 was sparked, in part, by slavery in North America. When the war was over, the Southern states promised to end racial segregation, but this promise was not fulfilled and so campaigners such as Malcolm X (page 14) and Martin Luther King Junior (page 16) campaigned and changed the course of black history forever.

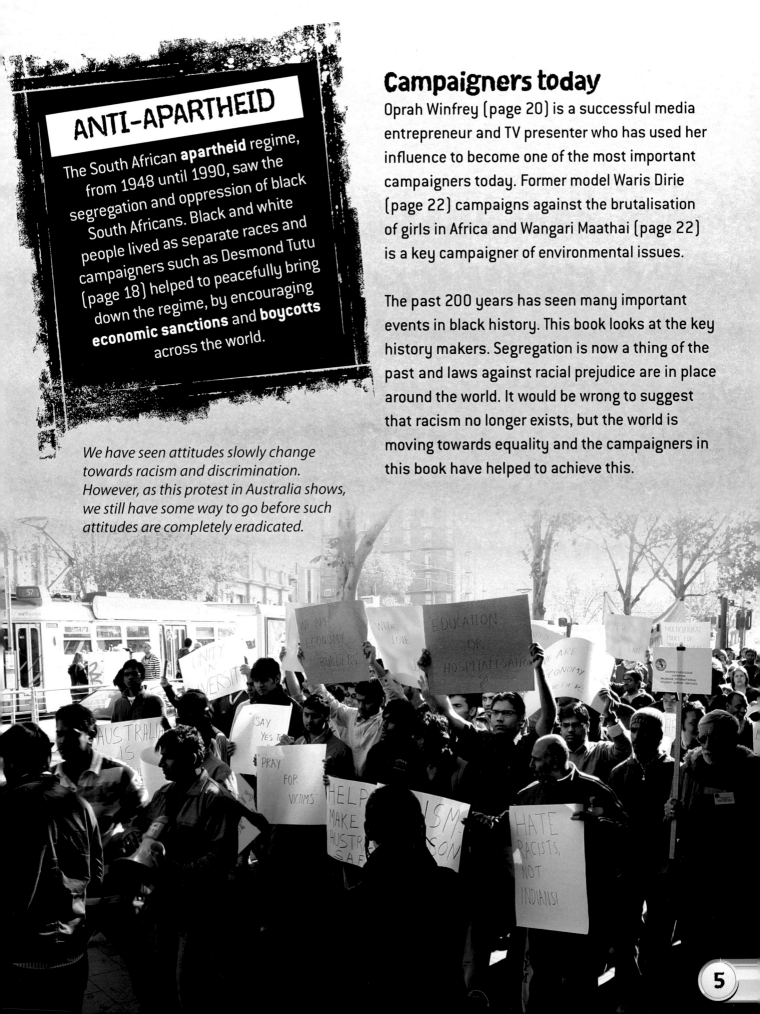

ANTI-APARTHEID

The South African **apartheid** regime, from 1948 until 1990, saw the segregation and oppression of black South Africans. Black and white people lived as separate races and campaigners such as Desmond Tutu (page 18) helped to peacefully bring down the regime, by encouraging **economic sanctions** and **boycotts** across the world.

We have seen attitudes slowly change towards racism and discrimination. However, as this protest in Australia shows, we still have some way to go before such attitudes are completely eradicated.

Campaigners today

Oprah Winfrey (page 20) is a successful media entrepreneur and TV presenter who has used her influence to become one of the most important campaigners today. Former model Waris Dirie (page 22) campaigns against the brutalisation of girls in Africa and Wangari Maathai (page 22) is a key campaigner of environmental issues.

The past 200 years has seen many important events in black history. This book looks at the key history makers. Segregation is now a thing of the past and laws against racial prejudice are in place around the world. It would be wrong to suggest that racism no longer exists, but the world is moving towards equality and the campaigners in this book have helped to achieve this.

Sojourner Truth
Feminist & Abolitionist

Born into slavery

Sojourner Truth was born Isabella Baumfree. She lived her young life as a slave on a farm in New York state, in the USA. Her slave owners treated her badly until, in 1827, she fled with her youngest child and escaped to freedom in New York City.

God's mission

At the age of 46, Isabella changed her name and, believing that God had given her a mission in life, set out on a journey to spread the truth about women's rights and the abolition of slavery.

A tireless campaign

In 1851, addressing a women's rights convention in Ohio, USA, Sojourner delivered a famous speech outlining women's inequalities with men. Over the next two decades, she spoke before hundreds of audiences and helped to recruit black soldiers for the Union Army. Sojourner campaigned tirelessly against segregation until the age of 75.

Name: Isabella Baumfree (changed her name at the age of 46)

Born: 1797, New York state, USA

Died: 1883

Honours and awards: First black woman to be honoured with a statue in Washington, USA (2009).

Interesting Fact: She was 6 feet tall and strong, so as a slave was given jobs normally done by men.

> 66 I cannot read a book, but I have as much muscle as any man and can do as much work as any man. I have plowed and reaped and husked and mowed. Can any man do more than that? 99

Sojourner Truth

During the US Civil War, Sojourner used the money raised by her lectures to buy food and clothing for black soldiers.

Harriet Tubman
Underground Railroad 'conductor'

Name: Araminta Ross (changed her name after marriage)

Born: 1820, Maryland, USA

Died: 10 March 1913

Honours and awards: Buried with military honours at Fort Hill Cemetery, Auburn, USA.

Interesting Fact: Harriet was often called 'Moses', after the biblical hero who led slaves to freedom in Egypt.

Troubled beginnings

Harriet Tubman was born into slavery. She was regularly beaten by her slave masters and at the age of 12 she was hit with a metal weight. This caused blackouts and headaches for the rest of her life.

Underground Railroad

At the age of 30, Harriet escaped to Philadelphia (where slavery was illegal) and joined a group known as the 'Underground Railroad'. This group helped slaves escape from the Southern states. The 'railroad' was a path that slaves travelled at night with the help of 'conductors' who guided them from one safe-house to another. Harriet helped hundreds of slaves flee to the North this way.

Civil War

When the US Civil War began in 1861, Harriet worked for the Union Army. She was the first woman to lead an armed raid and freed more than 700 slaves at a battle at the Combahee River in South Carolina, USA. Harriet continued to campaign for the freedom of African Americans until her death in 1913.

During the US Civil War, Harriet worked for the Union Army as a cook, a nurse and a spy!

> **"** I freed a thousand slaves. I could have freed a thousand more if only they knew they were slaves. **"**
>
> *Harriet Tubman*

Mary Seacole
The War Nurse

Name: Mary Jane Seacole (nee Grant)

Born: 1805, Kingston, Jamaica

Died: 14 May 1881

Honours and awards: A statue in her honour will be unveiled outside St Thomas's hospital, London, UK, in 2015.

Interesting Fact: Mary treated the Prince of Wales (Queen Victoria's son) when he was sick.

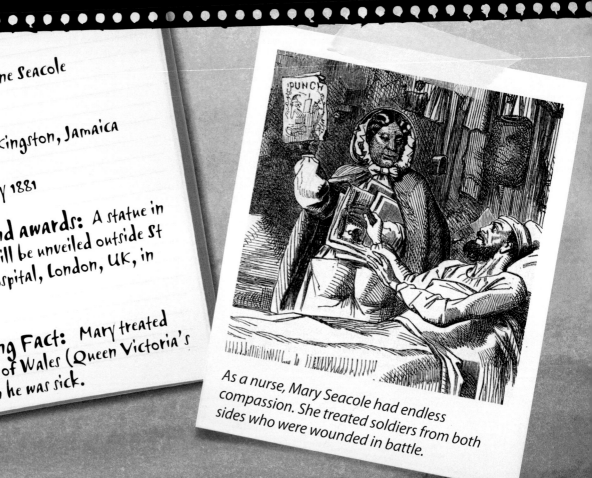

As a nurse, Mary Seacole had endless compassion. She treated soldiers from both sides who were wounded in battle.

Healing hands

When Mary was born in 1805, Jamaica was a British **colony**. Her father was a soldier in the Army and her mother was a 'healer' who treated British soldiers with her herbal medicines. As a girl, Mary practised bandaging her dolls and by the age of 12 was helping her mother treat the injured men.

Nursing the sick

In 1850, there was an outbreak of the disease **cholera** in Jamaica. Though not a trained nurse, Mary cared for many cholera victims, giving them her home-made herbal remedies.

Then, in 1851, she travelled to Panama in South America. In the mosquito-ridden jungle, Mary bravely rolled up her sleeves and got to work, caring for victims of cholera and **yellow fever**.

The Crimean War

In 1854, the Crimean War broke out in Russia. Mary asked the British Government to fund her trip to the Crimea to help nurse the wounded, but when they refused (Mary suspected it was on the grounds of her race), she funded her own trip. In 1855, she set sail for the Crimea.

A portrait of Mary Seacole painted in about 1869. It now hangs in the National Portrait Gallery, London, UK.

In the Crimea, Mary set up a store with a little hospital above it. The store sold home-cooked food and upstairs she cleaned wounds and applied bandages. On the battlefields, she treated the injured with no concern for the danger around her, often treating soldiers while under gunfire.

Returning home

When she returned to England, Mary was in ill-health and very poor, so the British press ran a campaign to raise money for her. Her nursing reputation rivalled that of Florence Nightingale and today Mary is still remembered as one of the world's most famous nurses.

MAKING HISTORY

Before the Crimean War, Britain had no trained nurses and nursing was not seen as a 'worthy' job. But Mary Seacole changed the way that people thought about nursing forever. In 1860, Britain's first training school for nurses was set up at St Thomas's Hospital in London.

Frederick Douglass
Inspirational Speaker

A haunting beginning

Frederick spent his early years with his grandmother, working as a slave. From a young age he witnessed the ill-treatment of slaves by their masters. At the age of 7, Frederick was separated from his grandmother and sent to live with his slave master.

Learning to read

Though it was illegal, when Frederick was about 12 years old, his slave mistress taught him to read. He began to read newspapers and books and soon his thoughts on human rights took shape. He started to understand how words could bring about positive change and so began to teach slaves on the plantation to read.

A great speaker

Frederick escaped slavery at the age of 20 by impersonating a sailor. He changed his name and began to campaign for the abolition of slavery. Despite being a nervous young man, at the age of 23 Frederick gave an eloquent speech about the life of a slave in front of hundreds of abolitionists. He continued to speak out against anti-slavery and women's rights until his death in 1895.

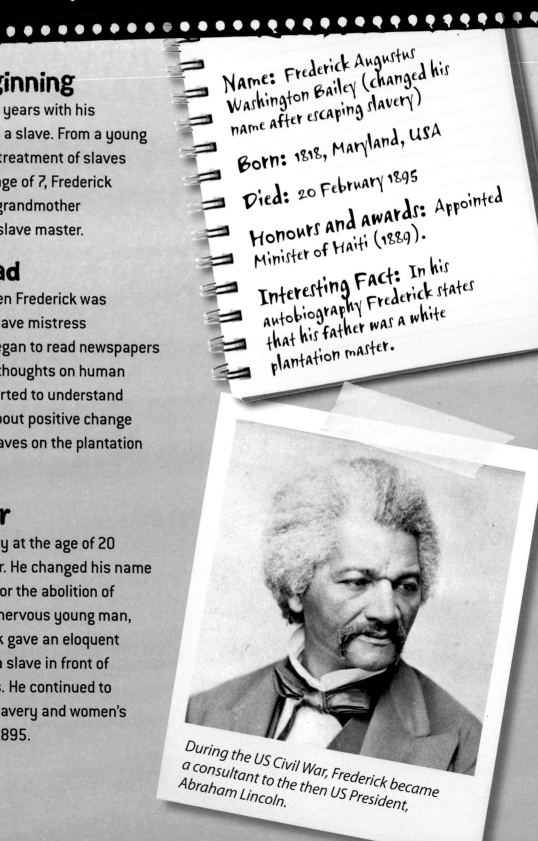

Name: Frederick Augustus Washington Bailey (changed his name after escaping slavery)

Born: 1818, Maryland, USA

Died: 20 February 1895

Honours and awards: Appointed Minister of Haiti (1889).

Interesting Fact: In his autobiography Frederick states that his father was a white plantation master.

During the US Civil War, Frederick became a consultant to the then US President, Abraham Lincoln.

Marcus Garvey
'Back to Africa' Movement

Name: Marcus Mosiah Garvey Junior

Born: 17 August 1887, Jamaica

Died: 10 June 1940

Honours and awards: National Hero of Jamaica (1964).

Interesting Fact: Garvey's beliefs influenced the **Rastafarian movement** and he is often mentioned in **reggae** music.

In 1919, Marcus set up an ocean liner company to transport black people from America, 'Back to Africa'.

Early life

Marcus Garvey was born in Jamaica, the youngest of 11 children. As he grew up, he became very aware of the racial discrimination in Jamaican society. This sparked Marcus's life-long interest in politics and social issues.

Leaving Jamaica

In 1910, Marcus left Jamaica to work on his uncle's banana plantation in Costa Rica. He saw how his fellow black people were being treated and resolved to change things.

In the early twentieth century, many African Americans were still experiencing poverty and prejudice. Marcus founded the Universal Negro Improvement Association (UNIA) to empower them. He argued that black people should unite and move back to Africa to form a powerful nation.

A radical speaker

Garvey had a **radical** approach to campaigning. His **inflammatory** speeches could cause crowd hysteria as he urged African Americans to return to Africa. Though he led a determined campaign throughout his life, Marcus never actually set foot in Africa himself.

Rosa Lee Parks
Mother of the Civil Rights Movement

Rosa Parks grew up on her grandparents' farm in Alabama, USA. The family was terrorised by a group of white **supremacists** called the **Ku Klux Klan**, who burned down homes and murdered innocent black people.

Family life was hard for Rosa, but she left the farm in 1924 when she enrolled at a private girls' school in Montgomery. There she began to train as a teacher. However, she was unable to graduate because she had to return home to look after her grandmother who had become unwell.

Name: Rosa Louise Parks (nee McCauley)

Born: 4 February 1913, Tuskegee, Alabama, USA

Died: 24 October 2005

Honours and awards: US Government Congressional Gold Medal (1999).

Interesting fact: When Rosa was young, she spent only five months of the year at school. The rest of the year she worked in the cotton fields.

Rosa Parks continued to campaign for racial equality until her death in 2005 at the age of 92.

The NAACP

Rosa married a civil rights worker called Raymond Parks in 1932 and together they joined the National Association for the Advancement of Colored People (NAACP), fighting for black people's right to vote.

After the US Civil War ended in 1865, the Southern states of America had promised to grant new freedoms to black people. However, racial segregation still existed, with separate 'black' and 'white' areas used in public facilities.

A re-enactment of that momentous day in 1955, when Rosa Parks stood up for what she believed in. Her act of defiance would change America forever.

Bus boycott

Both Rosa and Raymond were active members of the NAACP but Rosa's greatest contribution to the civil rights movement happened on 1 December, 1955. At that time, the Montgomery bus company segregated black and white people with separate seating areas, but black people were often required to stand. On that day, the bus driver asked Rosa to stand to allow a white passenger to sit down. When Rosa refused she was arrested and jailed.

Law changes

On 5 December, with the help of a young civil rights activist called Martin Luther King Junior (page 16), the black people of Montgomery, USA, decided to stand up for their rights. They began a boycott of the bus system which lasted 381 days, until Rosa's case was decided in the US Supreme Court. The outcome went in their favour and from that day on it became illegal to separate black and white people on buses.

Malcolm X
Radical Black Nationalist

Name: Malcolm Little (changed his surname to X in 1952)

Born: 19 May 1925, Nebraska, USA

Died: 21 February 1965

Honours and awards: His life has been portrayed in print and on stage and screen, including *The Autobiography of Malcolm X* by Alex Hayley and Spike Lee's 1992 film *Malcolm X*.

Interesting fact: Malcolm was always very smart and well-groomed, and after his troubled early days, he never smoked or drank alcohol.

After his assassination in 1965, Malcolm X became a cult figure, particularly among the black youth of America.

Early memories

One of Malcolm Little's earliest memories was watching his family home burn down. The Ku Klux Klan terrorised his family and when his father was killed in 1931, it was rumoured that the Klan were to blame. With his father no longer around, the young Malcolm fell in with the wrong crowd and ended up involved with gamblers and thieves. In 1946, he was jailed for 10 years.

Moving on

In prison, Malcolm discovered the Nation of Islam. This Muslim group believed in the superiority of black people over white people. Upon his release, Malcolm began to give fiery speeches and became the group's leader in 1952. He was critical of white America and preached black **supremacy**, believing that part of the USA should become a separate nation for black people. He encouraged African Americans to use violence against white people to regain their position in society.

> " The common goal of 22 million Afro-Americans is respect as human beings, the God-given right to be a human being. Our common goal is to obtain the human rights that America has been denying us. "

Malcolm X, 25 August 1964

A change of heart

But in 1964, Malcolm's beliefs changed. His new idea was that all races should try to live together peacefully. He travelled through the Middle East and Africa, preaching peace. However, many of his old followers disagreed with his new ideas and, in February 1965, he was **assassinated** while attending a rally in New York.

Malcolm urged his followers to defend themselves 'by any means necessary'. Here, he is addressing a crowd at a black Muslim rally in New York, 1963.

MAKING HISTORY

Malcolm X raised **black consciousness** among African Americans, reconnecting them with their African heritage and encouraging them to take control of their lives. From the late 1980s onwards, Malcolm X became an icon in black music and pop culture when a group of conscious black rappers began to use his image on album covers and music videos.

Martin Luther King
Civil Rights Hero

A good start

Michael King Junior was born in 1929 and grew up in relative wealth compared to many African Americans. He wanted to be a minister as he thought it was a strong position from which to fight racism. He became the pastor of a church in Montgomery, Alabama and it was here that he showed the first signs of being a great inspirational public speaker.

Southern states

Before the 1950s, segregation was in force in the Southern states of America. Black people attended different schools, were segregated on buses and attended different restaurants and cinemas. The civil rights movement began in 1951 to fight this inequality and Martin Luther King became one of its most influential leaders.

Bus boycott

In 1955, Martin became President of the Montgomery Improvement Association (MIA). The organisation supported Rosa Lee Parks (page 12) who was arrested for failing to give up her seat to a white passenger. The MIA led the 'Montgomery Bus Boycott', forcing a change in the law and making it illegal to segregate black and white passengers.

Name: Michael King Junior (later changed his name to Martin Luther)

Born: 15 January 1929, Atlanta, Georgia, USA

Died: 4 April 1968

Honours and awards: 1964 Nobel Peace Prize.

Interesting fact: He deeply admired Gandhi, the Indian leader who fought against British rule in India in a peaceful and non-violent way.

Martin Luther King believed and encouraged non-violent protest, through boycotts, demonstrations and freedom marches.

Assassination

Martin's views on non-violent protest were not popular with everyone. Many African Americans thought more extreme action was needed. Meanwhile, white supremacists took to firebombing his house. The day after a passionate demonstration in support of a strike in Tennessee, he was shot and killed while standing on a hotel balcony. His body now lies in the Martin Luther King Junior Centre for Non-Violent Social Change.

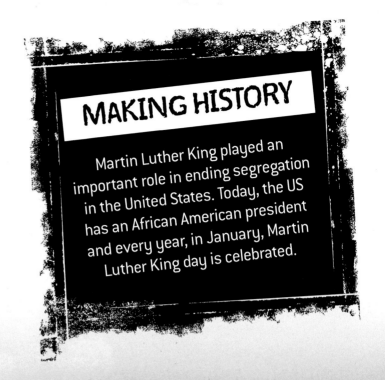

MAKING HISTORY

Martin Luther King played an important role in ending segregation in the United States. Today, the US has an African American president and every year, in January, Martin Luther King day is celebrated.

In August 1963, Martin Luther King gave his 'I have a dream' speech in Washington D.C., USA, to a crowd of 200,000 people.

Archbishop Desmond Tutu
Anti-apartheid Activist

A tolerant family

Desmond Tutu was born in Klerksdorp, South Africa. His father was a teacher and his mother a domestic worker. He was raised in a tolerant, peace-loving home. At the age of 12, Tutu's family moved to Johannesburg. At school, he wanted to be a doctor but his family could not afford it, so instead he trained as a teacher.

Full name: Desmond Mpilo Tutu

Born: 7 October 1931, Transvaal, South Africa

Honours and awards: First black Archbishop of Cape Town (1984). Nobel Peace Prize for helping to defeat apartheid (1984). Presidential Medal of Freedom (2009).

Interesting fact: In 1975, Desmond Tutu was appointed Dean of St. Mary's Cathedral in Johannesburg, South Africa. He was the first black person to hold the position.

Desmond Tutu put forward the idea of South Africa as the 'Rainbow Nation' in which all races would live in peace.

> **"** Never will white people hear what we are trying to say? Please, all we are asking you to do is to recognise that we are humans, too. **"**
>
> *Desmond Tutu*

Religion

Tutu decided he didn't want to teach and in 1958 he left the profession to study theology. He was ordained as an Anglican minister in 1961 and eventually became Archbishop of Cape Town in 1986.

Anti-apartheid

In 1978, Desmond became the general secretary of the South African Council of Churches. In this role he was a leading spokesman for the rights of black South Africans. The apartheid regime, introduced in 1948, meant that black and white South Africans were required to live separately. Black people were not allowed to vote or travel and interracial marriage was illegal.

In the 1980s, Desmond Tutu spoke out against apartheid, bringing the world's attention to the suffering of black South Africans. He encouraged non-violent action to stop the regime and an economic boycott of South Africa.

Throughout the 1980s Desmond Tutu travelled around the world, speaking out against apartheid.

Soon many countries of the world were putting economic pressure on the South African government to abolish apartheid.

Voice of peace

Desmond used his position to speak out against apartheid and today he is a powerful voice for peace and justice all over the world.

MAKING HISTORY

Tutu was highly influential in bringing down the apartheid system. He encouraged economic sanctions from countries all over the world, forcing the South African government to make changes to the law. As a result of these changes, in 1990 Nelson Mandela was released from prison after almost 27 years.

Oprah Winfrey
Modern Campaigner

Oprah was an intelligent child who, even at the young age of three, loved to be on stage and sing in church. However, Oprah suffered sexual abuse in the family home and at the age of nine she ran away. She became pregnant at 14 years of age but her son died in infancy.

Name: Oprah Gail Winfrey

Born: 29 January 1954, Mississippi, USA

Honours and awards: Featured in *Time* magazine's annual listing: '100 Most Influential People in the World' from 2004 onwards.

Interesting fact: Oprah's appearance in the film of Alice Walker's book, *The Color Purple* (1985), earned her an Oscar nomination.

One of America's most-loved TV celebrities, Oprah's commitment to the education and empowerment of women and children is tireless and ongoing.

Career takes off

Oprah's broadcasting career began at 17 years of age when she was employed by a Nashville radio station to read the news. Her warm, emotional style led her to be offered the opportunity to host a daytime talk show. It was this step which marked the beginning of her television career and, in 1985, *The Oprah Winfrey Show* began. A year later it was the number one television show in America.

Oprah's Angel Network

Since the early 1990s, Oprah has campaigned in favour of a database of convicted abusers. In 1998, she set up Oprah's Angel Network to encourage TV viewers to 'use their lives' to help others. The Network raised $80 million and has funded good causes all over the world.

Leadership for girls

Oprah established her Leadership Academy Foundation during a visit to South Africa in 2002. In 2007, she opened a state-of-the-art school that fosters high standards of achievement for girls from impoverished backgrounds. She has also pledged funds to South African orphanages and rural schools, with 50,000 children receiving food, clothing, books and toys. Oprah was the first African American woman to become a billionaire. She is now using her fame and wealth to support and help people all over the world.

Oprah talks to students at the Oprah Winfrey Leadership Academy for Girls in Gauteng, South Africa, 2009.

> " It doesn't matter who you are or where you come from. The ability to triumph begins with you. Always. "
>
> *Oprah Winfrey*

MAKING HISTORY

The 1993 'Oprah Bill' was passed, establishing a database of convicted child abusers which is now available to law enforcement agencies across America. Her charitable projects and grants continue to support women, children and families across the world.

Other Campaigners

Jesse Jackson (1941-)

Born in South Carolina, USA, as a child Jesse was teased for having 'no daddy'. He went on to win a scholarship to Chicago University and hoped to escape the discrimination of the South. He became a leader in the civil rights movement, encouraging protests and boycotts. Jackson travelled the USA promising a 'rainbow coalition' of black and white people.

Booker T Washington (1856-1915)

Booker Taliaferro Washington was born a slave in the USA. He believed that education was the passport to economic freedom and social equality and so he campaigned tirelessly to reform and improve education for black Americans. In 1881, he started an adult education college in Alabama to train black Americans as future teachers and farmers.

Mary Bethune (1875-1955)

Born to former slaves in South Carolina, USA, Mary McLeod Bethune became one of the great educators in United States history. At a time when there was little or no education for black people, she single-handedly set up a school in Daytona Beach, Florida to teach African American girls. She had no equipment and was forced to use crates as desks, and crush berries to make ink for writing. To help raise funds, Mary and the pupils baked pies to sell. The school grew with the help of investors and today it is known as the Bethune-Cookman College. It now has more than 1,000 students.

Wangari Maathai (1940-2011)

Known as the 'tree woman', Wangari Maathai was raised in a Kenyan village. In 1976, she founded the Green Belt Movement. This required women from the villages to plant trees to protect the Kenyan landscape. Her actions had a positive effect on the environment and on the local women, who saw that positive action could change things. In 2002, Wangari was elected to parliament and worked with the United Nations on environmental issues and improving education.

Waris Dirie (1965-)

As a teenager, Somali model, actress, writer and activist Waris Dirie fled from Somalia to London to avoid an arranged marriage. She worked at McDonald's before starting a modelling career. In 1997, she began to campaign for an end to female genital mutilation and was appointed United Nations Special Ambassador for the cause. In 2009, she co-founded the Foundation for Women's Dignity and Rights and raises money for schools and clinics in her native Somalia.

Timeline

Legacy

1850-60 The Underground Railway system helps free thousands of black slaves

1854 The Crimean War begins

1860 St Thomas's hospital in London sets up Britain's first nursing school

1861-65 The US Civil War

1865 Slavery is officially abolished in the USA

1925 Malcolm X is born

1929 Martin Luther King Junior is born

1948 The system of apartheid begins in South Africa

1951 Start of the civil rights movement in USA

1955 Rosa Parks refuses to give up her bus seat

1955-56 The Montgomery Bus Boycott

1960s The start of the Black Power movement, a movement which emphasised racial pride

1962 Nelson Mandela is imprisoned

1963 Martin Luther King's 'I have a dream...' speech, Washington D.C., USA

1965 The assassination of Malcolm X

1968 The assassination of Martin Luther King Junior

1990 Nelson Mandela is released from prison and the apartheid regime collapses in South Africa

1994 Democratic elections are held for all South African people

2008 Barack Obama is voted the first African American President of the United States of America. He was re-elected for a second term in 2012

The legacies of the campaigners in this book live on, not only in their achievements but also through the work of their families and followers:

Malcolm X Memorial Foundation: www.malcolmxfoundation.org/wp
Founded in 1971 to commemorate his life and work.

Mary Seacole Statue: http://www.maryseacoleappeal.org.uk/
The memorial appeal for the upcoming statue outside St. Thomas's Hospital in London, UK to recognise all the work Mary did in her lifetime.

Tutu Foundation UK: http://www.tutufoundationuk.org/
This foundation continues Tutu's work by increasing tolerance and understanding in society and creating links between different cultures.

Glossary

BETTWS 23/10/14

Abolitionist A campaigner who wants to get rid of slavery.

Apartheid A government policy that promoted the separation of black and white people.

Assassination To murder a prominent figure.

Black consciousness A movement seeking to unite black people and take pride in the black race.

Boycott To refuse to deal with a country or organisation as a form of protest.

Cholera A disease caused by drinking dirty water.

Colony A country under the rule of another country.

Economic sanction When a country puts trade and financial restrictions on another country.

Inflammatory Intended to arouse anrgy or violent feelings.

Ku Klux Klan A secret society of white southerners in the USA, who terrorise and suppress black people.

Oppression Exerting a form of power over another group.

Petition A written document, signed by a lot of people, to try to demand action from a government or other authority.

Plantation A large estate or farm where crops are grown and tended to by workers.

Radical A person with extreme views.

Rastafarian movement A form of religion that originated in Jamaica and regards the Emperor of Ethiopia (Haile Selassie or 'Ras Tafari') as God.

Reggae A style of music, originating in Jamaica.

Segregation To separate or set apart.

Supremacy Having the highest power or authority.

Supremacist A person who believes in the supreme power of a particular group.

Yellow fever A deadly virus, passed on by mosquitoes.

Index